A simple machines timeline

5500 BC

Chinese farmers start to use stone ploughshares to break up the ground.

3100 BC

In England, Stone Age builders use wedges and levers to shift massive stones and build Stonehenge.

3500 BC

The wheel is invented. Its first use is as a potter's wheel.

2630-2611 BC

The ancient Egyptians use levers, wedges and screws (simple drills) to build the first pyramid.

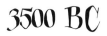

c. 1440

The printing press is invented in Europe. Access to books spreads rapidly.

2016

For the first time, a tool is 3-D printed in outer space. It is a multi-tool, including a wedge.

1763

James Watt begins developing a steam engine that can drive a piston.

c. AD 1000

The spinning wheel is invented in India, making it much easier to make yarn and fabric.

1879

Karl Benz patents an internal combustion engine and uses it to power a car.

1760–1830

The Industrial Revolution sees a huge increase in mechanisation, with machines introduced in many industries.

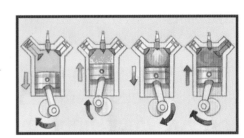

Origins of simple machines

United States:
3-D printer

Scotland:
Steam engine

Iraq: Archimedes' screw

China and
Iran: Windmills

Iraq, Georgia
(Eurasia):
Wheels used for
transportation

India:
Spinning wheel

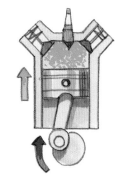

Germany: Internal
combustion engine

Africa: Earliest
humans use levers
and wedges

China: Wedges
used as plows

It's impossible to say exactly where some simple machines were first used. The earliest humans probably used wedges and sticks as simple levers about 185,000 years ago. Other simple machines were first used at about the same time in different places around the world. It is only in the case of more advanced machines, comprising several parts, that we have a better idea of where and when they were first used.

Author:

Anne Rooney has a PhD in English from the University of Cambridge. She is the author of many books for children and adults, specialising in science and technology topics.

Artist:

Mark Bergin was born in Hastings, England, in 1961. He studied at Eastbourne College of Art and specialises in historical reconstructions, aviation and maritime subjects. He lives in Bexhill-on-Sea with his wife and children.

Editor: **Jonathan Ingoldby**

Editorial Assistant: **Mark Williams**

PAPER FROM
SUSTAINABLE
FORESTS

Published in Great Britain in MMXVIII by Book House, an imprint of
The Salariya Book Company Ltd
25 Marlborough Place, Brighton BN1 1UB
www.salariya.com

ISBN: 978-1-912537-08-2

3 5 7 9 8 6 4 2

A CIP catalogue record for this book is available from the British Library.
Printed and bound in Malaysia.
Reprinted in MMXIX.

Visit
www.salariya.com
for our online catalogue and
free fun stuff.

You Wouldn't Want to Live Without™

Simple Machines!

Written by
Anne Rooney

Illustrated by
Mark Bergin

BOOK HOUSE
a SALARIYA *imprint*

Contents

Introduction

Simple machines are all around us and we use them every day, often without thinking. Some of them are so simple you probably don't even recognise them as machines. How about a knife? A hammer? Tweezers? They all count as *simple machines*! Many simple machines are hidden inside complex devices, called *compound machines* – but the simple machines are still in there, doing their job. You'll be surprised at how many simple machines you use every day – you really wouldn't want to live without them!

What is a machine?

A machine is a mechanical device or tool that uses energy to control or produce movement. That might sound rather complicated, but it just means that a machine is something that helps you to move things. To be useful, a machine must make a task easier. It does this by amplifying – increasing the effect of – a force. Machines can be simple, working on just one type of force or movement, or they can be complicated.

MORE COMPLICATED machines, such as car engines, are known as compound machines. They incorporate many, many simple machines working together.

TO SCIENTISTS, *work* has a very specific meaning: it's the energy it takes to exert a force over a distance. That means thinking about a hard maths problem isn't work, but playing football is!

Drag – air in the way of the bird slows it down.

Lift – air underneath pushes the bird up.

Thrust – the work done by the bird's muscles pushes it forwards.

Gravity – the bird's weight pulls it down.

MOVEMENT is produced and controlled by forces (pushes or pulls). If we know the forces involved, we can work out just how an object will move. Often, there are several forces working at once – it can get tricky!

How it works

Your body works like a machine: it takes energy from food and uses it so that your muscles can do 'work'. It has lots of parts that work as simple machines.

A MACHINE increases the effect of a force. Without machines, we'd have to rely on our own raw strength to move everything. This would mean we could move small things, but would really struggle to move anything bigger.

SOME MACHINES are better than others at helping you out. When a force is amplified by a machine it gives you *mechanical advantage*. The greater the mechanical advantage, the more like a super-hero you get to be!

It's simple!

You might usually think of a machine as a complicated metal thing with lots of moving parts, like a car or a washing machine. But to physicists it can be something much simpler than that.

It doesn't need to be complicated, or metal, and it doesn't even need to have any parts that move on their own.

There are five types of simple machine, meaning basic mechanical devices that help to apply a force. We use them every day in lots of different ways. They are: lever, pulley, screw, wheel and axle, and wedge and inclined plane.

EVEN A DRAWING PIN is a simple machine!

Pulley

Screw

Lever

Wheel

Wedge

Inclined plane

Keep your bicycle, scooter, skateboard or roller skates well-oiled so the parts move smoothly with little friction.

LOTS OF simple machines don't look like 'machines' at all. A spade is a machine; so is the screw lid of a jar, a nail, a hammer and even a plank balanced on a box.

Oil rig

Racing car

SIMPLE machines can be combined to make a compound machine. These can be very complicated, like an oil rig or a racing car.

I'll try a spot of friction!

FRICTION is a force that operates between moving surfaces. Rougher surfaces produce more friction. Friction produces heat, which is why working machines get hot.

SOME MACHINES (left) work more effectively than our bodies, wasting less energy as heat. A bicycle uses the work of your muscles more efficiently than running does.

13

Putting machines to work

Our earliest ancestors must have made use of some forms of simple machines while still living in caves. Other simple machines, such as wheels and pulleys, that needed to be constructed would have come later. Simple machines made human civilisation possible. They enabled people to make buildings, dig the soil, water crops, move around, make fabrics and tools – and even fight each other.

USING A STRONG stick as a lever makes it easier to move a really heavy stone. Look above you!

SOME simple machines are so obvious, even animals use them. Some birds use sticks as levers. The nuthatch uses one to lift tree bark to uncover insects hidden beneath.

Something's not right . . .

A SHADOOF consists of a bucket attached to a stick that pivots so that the water can be scooped up. Tools like this made the job of watering crops much easier.

It's easier to move something up a slope than to lift it vertically, and it's safer to move something down a slope than to drop it off an edge.

WHEELS (left) were invented in various places around the same time, about 5,500 years ago. They made it much easier to move things and people.

WEDGES, ramps, levers and pulleys (right) helped people to build huge structures such as Stonehenge in England and the pyramids in Egypt.

ARCHIMEDES' screw (left) has been used for at least 2,700 years. Turning the screw scoops up water and raises it up the screw shaft.

A PLOUGHSHARE (right) is wedge-shaped to cut through the soil, making a furrow (dip) for seeds to be sown in a neat row. Ploughs have been used for 5,500 years.

Much better than a bucket!

Archimedes' screw

15

It's not all fun and games

A lever is essentially some form of stick used in a clever way. Using a lever helps you to move or lift an object that is too heavy. It increases the effect of your effort, making the force applied much stronger. Without simple machines like levers, we'd never be able to move anything heavier than we can lift or push. Imagine all the things we couldn't do!

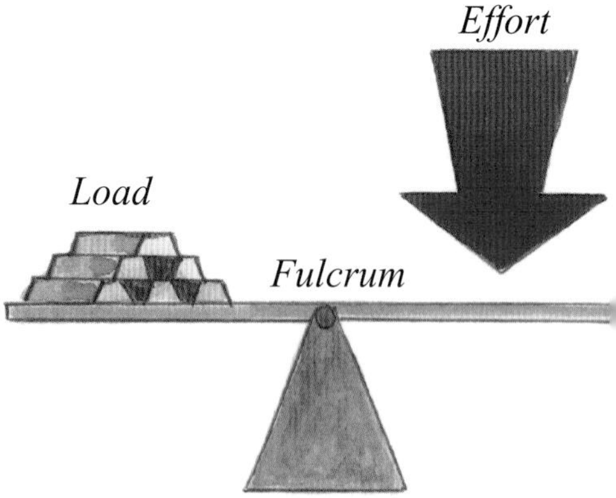

Effort

Load

Fulcrum

LEVERS USE effort exerted at one point to move a load at another point. The point around which the lever moves is called the fulcrum.

Anybody got any bright ideas?

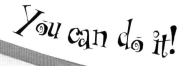

You can do it!

Make a model see-saw and experiment by varying the positions and size of the load, and the effort. What happens if you move the fulcrum off centre and towards one end?

A SEE-SAW is a class 1 lever. Each person on a see-saw provides both load and effort. More effort on one side can raise the load too much!

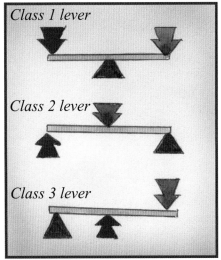

Class 1 lever

Class 2 lever

Class 3 lever

TWEEZERS give no mechanical advantage as the effort and load are on the same side. As a class 3 lever, they're useful for making precise movements.

THERE ARE three types of lever (left). They vary according to where the fulcrum is in relation to the lever. You can find out more about them on pages 37 and 39.

JAWS are a pair of levers that work together, like super-snappy scissors. The top and bottom jaws exert force in opposite directions.

Effort   *Fulcrum*

A WHEELBARROW is a class 2 lever. The effort and load both move in the same direction – up.

The wheels on the bus

Wheels are much easier to recognise than many other types of simple machines! The centre of one or more wheels are attached to a rod (called the axle), so that both the wheel and the axle turn together. Wheels and axles can work in either of two ways. We can apply a force to the rim of the wheel to turn the axle, or we can apply a force to the axle to turn the wheel. Wheels often come in pairs, one at each end of an axle.

IT'S EASIER to move a box on a trolley than to drag it over the ground. Wheels reduce the area in contact with the ground, so there is less friction.

THE OUTER EDGE of a wheel moves much further than the centre. The bigger the wheel, the further the vehicle moves with each turn.

Slowcoach!

Use a construction toy to make a vehicle with wheels and axles. If you have a selection of wheels, experiment with different sizes.

A MERRY-GO-ROUND is a giant wheel-and-axle system. The centre section turns more slowly than the outside, so don't choose a ride near the edge unless you like to go fast!

COGS OR GEARS are wheels with teeth that lock into the teeth of another wheel. When one turns, it turns another.

THE INVENTION of the wheel made people more productive. A horse-drawn wagon can move ten times more than one person can over the same distance and in the same amount of time.

THE PEOPLE of the early civilisations in South America lived without wheels. Perhaps they didn't invent wheels because they had no large, strong animals to pull carts!

19

Ups and downs

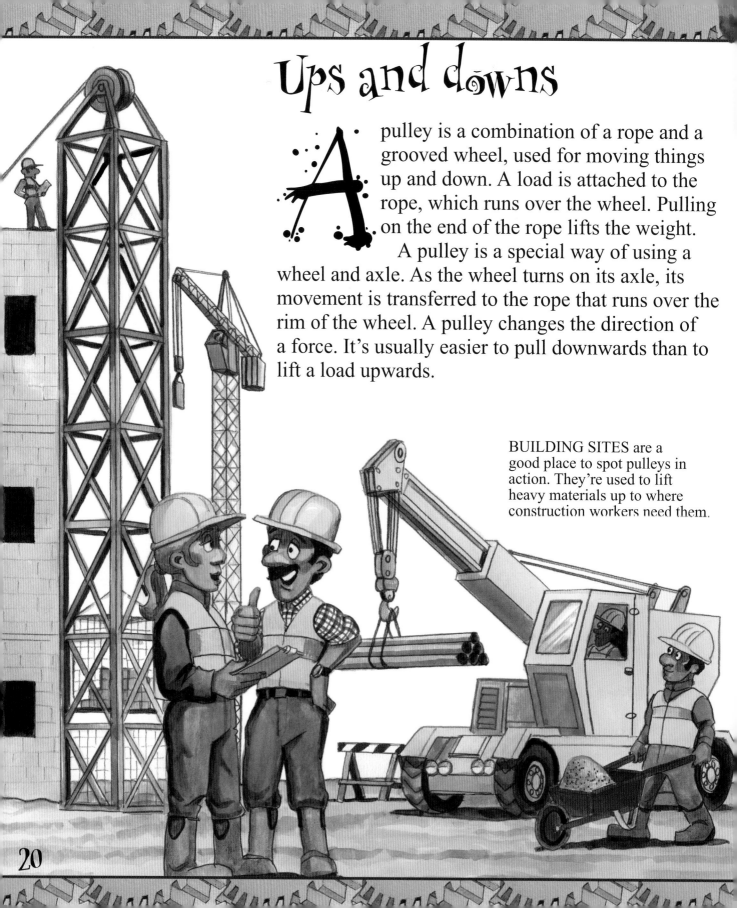

A pulley is a combination of a rope and a grooved wheel, used for moving things up and down. A load is attached to the rope, which runs over the wheel. Pulling on the end of the rope lifts the weight.

A pulley is a special way of using a wheel and axle. As the wheel turns on its axle, its movement is transferred to the rope that runs over the rim of the wheel. A pulley changes the direction of a force. It's usually easier to pull downwards than to lift a load upwards.

BUILDING SITES are a good place to spot pulleys in action. They're used to lift heavy materials up to where construction workers need them.

20

Older lifts (elevators) work using a pulley. A counterweight balances the weight of the lift and as one goes up, the other goes down.

A SIMPLE pulley (above) doesn't reduce the effort needed to move a load, but it makes a task feel much easier.

SAILORS move heavy sails using a block and tackle system (below) – two or more linked pulleys with a rope running through both.

PULLEYS ARE used to haul water from a well. It's easier to pull a rope over a pulley than just to pull it over a beam or branch, because there's less friction. And it's a lot easier than climbing down to the water every time.

A slippery slope

The first wedges were used thousands of years ago. A wedge is a triangular shape with a fat end that tapers to a point. It can be used to separate, lift or to hold something in place. When a downwards face is applied to the fat end of a wedge, its slanted sides change the direction of the force into one that pushes outwards instead of down. This sideways force separates things. Using the slanted side of a wedge as a ramp or inclined plane makes it easier to move something up or down. If you whizz down a slide, you're having fun with a wedge shape.

The best wedge shape ever!

A NARROW wedge is easier to drive into a small gap – but it has to move further to have the same effect as a wider wedge.

WEDGES HAVE been used for thousands of years for breaking apart tough materials. The massive stones used to build the Egyptian pyramids were cut in this way.

It needs another good whack!

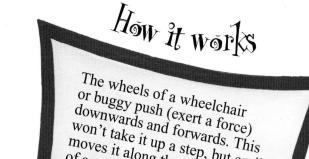

The wheels of a wheelchair or buggy push (exert a force) downwards and forwards. This won't take it up a step, but easily moves it along the sloping surface of a ramp.

MOST CUTTING tools are wedges (above). They slide between particles of material where a blunt edge would just crush the matter beneath it.

WOODEN wedges were once driven into rock and soaked with water to split rock (left). As the wedge swells, the rock is forced apart. If the water freezes, it works even better – ice takes up more space than water, so the wedge becomes bigger.

WEDGES can also be used to keep things in place. A doorstop is a wedge placed between the floor and the bottom of the door to keep it open (left). A nail is a wedge that pushes apart the fabric of a wall or a piece of wood.

YOUR MOUTH is full of wedges – look at the shape of your front teeth (right)! Jaw muscles force your wedge-teeth into food, breaking it into pieces.

All screwed up

A screw is made of metal. It has a shaft with a spiral wrapped around it. It converts rotational (round and round) movement to linear (straight line) movement. Turning a screw moves its shaft in a straight line. The screwdriver turns the screwhead, which turns the screw, which moves forwards into a surface. All screws aren't the same: screw threads can be on the outside or on the inside as on the lids of screw top jars.

THE THREAD of a wood screw has sharp edges. This acts like a blade or wedge, pushing its way into the wood. The sides of the thread help to push it forwards. If it meets something too hard, the screw locks – it doesn't go backwards.

Screw thread

ANIMALS CAN'T make screws, but some can learn to use them! Octopuses have been filmed unscrewing a jar to get at a tasty snack inside.

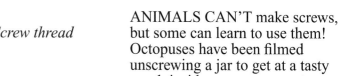

24

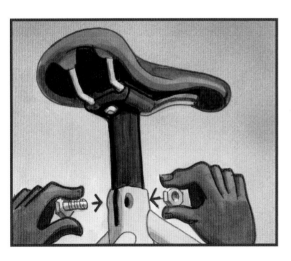

SCREWS WORK alone, but bolts are always paired with nuts. The bolt goes into a hole and then a nut with a matching thread is screwed onto the end of it.

A CAR JACK uses a screw to separate the car from the road surface (right). How would you change a tyre if you couldn't lift the car? The jack makes it simple. Your muscle power is enough to turn a screw that separates the arms of the jack, and the car on top is pushed upwards. Easy!

IF ALL SCREWS suddenly vanished, lots of things would just fall apart: furniture, buildings, vehicles. Screws are often hidden, but they serve a really useful purpose.

How did that happen?

SCREWS CAN BE used to pull two surfaces together and crush or press whatever is between them. In a press used to make olive oil or wine, a huge screw is used to lower a wide, flat plate into a barrel of olives or grapes, squashing them until the juice leaks out.

Putting it together

Simple machines aren't just used on their own. A complex – or compound – machine is made from simple machines working together. It can use just a few simple machines, or hundreds, as components.

Compound machines can amplify a force, change the direction of a force, change the type of energy and change the type of motion. They can change one kind of motion into another, sometimes going through several other kinds of motion on the way. There are four types of motion: linear, rotary, reciprocating and oscillating.

LINEAR MOTION is movement in a straight line, like a toy car moving forwards.

A BICYCLE is a compound machine. The gears transfer motion to the wheels. They go round (rotary motion) and the bicycle goes forwards (linear motion).

Don't forget my contribution!

BRAKES are levers. They move the brake blocks against the wheel (a linear movement) to stop the rotary motion of the wheel.

ROTARY motion goes in circles, like the wheel of a unicycle. The cyclist presses down on the pedals to turn the wheel.

How it works

Every compound machine has a source of energy, and mechanisms to produce and change forces and motions. Most machines also have some kind of user interface.

RECIPROCATING motion (right) goes backwards and forwards, like a saw cutting through wood. The teeth of the saw are tiny wedges that force their way into the wood.

IN A COMPOUND machine, the force produced by one simple machine becomes the starting force for the next (below). Force can be transformed repeatedly. Each component can make a change to the force or motion. Parts can be put together in inventive and imaginative ways.

OSCILLATING motion (above) is swinging from side to side, like a pendulum in a clock. Oscillating motion can be fun!

27

World-changing machines

Simple machines helped people to farm, build and make societies. They got us started! No one needed to understand how levers, wheels and wedges worked in order to use them. But then scientists and engineers began to explore the wider possibilities of machines. Soon, their understanding of how machines could work and putting them together into compound machines revolutionised societies. Without machines, we would have none of the benefits of farming and industrialisation. Life would be very different if these machines had never been developed.

A life of leisure... with all these modern machines.

THE INVENTION of the printing press around 1440 made books easily available, and knowledge soon spread rapidly. Without levers and screws, all books would still be hand-written.

CLOCKWORK is used for clocks and mechanisms, including automata and toys. Without wheels for clockwork, our ancestors would not have been able to measure time accurately.

INVENTED in India 1,000 years ago, a spinning wheel pulls yarn from a bundle of wool. Invented in 1764, the Spinning Jenny could make many threads at once, which revolutionised fabric-making.

How it works

WINDMILL

Grain fed in

Rotation

Wind

Floating stone

Rotary stone

Drive shaft

THE WIND turns a windmill's sails, attached to a shaft, which turns a gear, which turns a spindle at right angles to it. That turns another shaft, which turns a stone. Windmills ground corn and wheat, so people could make bread.

THE INDUSTRIAL REVOLUTION saw a shift from manual work (people working with their hands and with simple machines) to more and more tasks being done by more complex, powered machines. It was good for business, but not always for the workers . . .

. . . MANY PEOPLE rebelled against machines taking their jobs and making their skills less valuable. Some workers even attacked and broke up the compound machines, but they needed to use simple machines to do so!

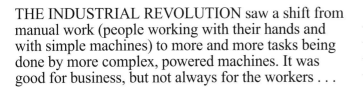

Power to the people

The first machines were powered by human or animal muscle power, or by the energy of wind or moving water. During the Industrial Revolution, extra power sources became available. Earlier machines were replaced by engines driven by steam, fuel and electricity. People (and animals) had to do a lot less physical work, and the new machines were faster and more efficient. They didn't get tired, need to sleep, get sick or go on holiday. Industry became much more productive, and societies flourished.

A WAGON and a train both use wheels, but a train can do much more work because it has more energy available to it.

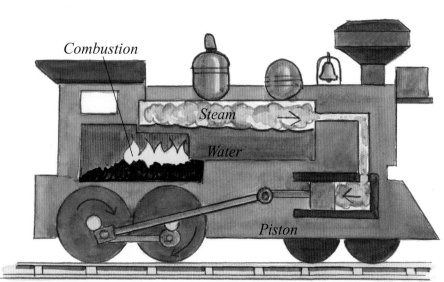

Combustion

Steam

Water

Piston

THE INDUSTRIAL REVOLUTION was largely powered by steam. The energy for a steam train comes from the pressure of boiling water in a closed space so that the steam pushes a piston. A steam train burned coal to heat water and provide steam pressure. This then drove pistons attached to cranks and transferred movement to the wheels to move the train along.

THE INTERNAL combustion engine (used in motor vehicles) takes energy from burning liquid fuel in a small space, using the pressure to drive a piston and so eventually turn the wheels.

We make electricity by turning a dense metal coil inside a magnetic field. When you use a wind-up torch, you're doing that directly. The electricity you make is stored in a battery.

ALESSANDRO Volta developed the first battery to produce electricity in 1799. Now lots of machines are powered by batteries. Imagine how different life would be without electricity!

POWER makes compound machines much more useful – but without simple machines, there wouldn't be any powered machines. We wouldn't be left with many transport options.

I'll never reach the cinema in time!

Would you want to live without simple machines?

If all the simple machines vanished overnight, there wouldn't be much technology left. Even things that aren't simple machines themselves are made using simple machines. We would have to find new – or old – ways of doing things that we currently take for granted. Life wouldn't be impossible, but it would be very different.

Luckily, simple machines aren't about to disappear. Instead, we will continue to find more and more ingenious and exciting uses for them.

WE DON'T notice some of the simple machines around us. The pointy nose of a fast train is a wedge, allowing it to move through the air much faster.

SIMPLE machines are all around us every day. Imagine how different life would be if we had to give them up.

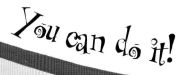

MOST VEHICLES use wheels and axles, and even those that don't run on wheels and use levers and pulleys for steering. Imagine riding a donkey to school? What would the donkey do all day?

SIMPLE machines (left) are being put to more and more complex uses. Without them, we wouldn't be making any technological progress. Who knows what they will be used for next?

MACHINES ARE taking over many difficult tasks. A bridge (right) that began construction in Amsterdam, Holland, in 2016, was put together entirely by robots from parts produced in metal using a 3-D printer.

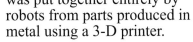

LOTS OF TOYS and activities depend on simple machines: merry-go-rounds, Ferris wheels, see-saws, swings, slides, roller blades, skateboards and more.

SOME MACHINES (right) seem to have hardly any mechanical parts. But simple machines are still needed to make them. There's no getting away from simple machines in the end!

33

Glossary

Amplify To make larger.

Automata (singular: automaton) Mechanical moving figures.

Axle The rod that runs through the middle of one or more wheels, providing the movement that turns the wheels.

Car jack A tool for lifting part of a car off the ground.

Civilisation The most advanced form of organised society, characterised by people building cities, developing communal projects and achieving advanced progress in science, technology and arts.

Compound machine A machine that has two or more simple machines among its components. A car is a good example.

Counterweight A heavy object that balances the weight of another part of a system.

Effort A force exerted by a machine or a person using a machine.

Force A push or a pull on an object, coming from its interaction with another object (or person).

Friction The force operating between two objects trying to move against each other. Friction resists movement and causes some of the energy in the system to be wasted as heat.

Fulcrum The pivoting or balancing point in a lever.

Inclined Slanted or tilted.

Industrial Revolution A period from around 1760 to 1830 which saw a very rapid increase in mechanisation and factory-building. People moved from manual work in small-scale industries to operating machines in large-scale industries, often leaving the countryside to live in cities.

Ingenious Clever and original.

Internal combustion engine An engine that burns fuel inside a sealed compartment, using the resulting pressure to move a piston.

Linear motion A movement in a straight line.

Load The weight that a machine is trying to move.

Mechanical Operated by some kind of machine.

Mechanical advantage The benefit gained by using a machine to do a task, measured as the force produced by a machine relative to the force applied to it.

Piston A plunger that fits closely inside a sealed compartment. It is moved by the pressure of compressed liquid or gas.

Printing press A machine that prints documents by pressing inked metal letters against a piece of paper.

Reciprocating motion A movement backward and forward.

Rotary motion A movement in circles, such as a wheel going round.

Shaft A long rod or pole to which something is fastened, or which forms the central part of a structure.

Stonehenge A circular structure made of huge chunks of shaped stone, some upright and some lying across the top of the uprights. It is near Salisbury in England, and was started around 5,100 years ago.

3-D printer A printer that makes a three-dimensional object, usually from plastic or metal.

Translate Convert into a different form or direction.

Work This is the process of transferring energy from one form or place to another. All simple machines do work.

Index

Amazing simple machines

Simple machines are so versatile that tools that look very similar can have very different uses. Think of a pair of scissors, a pair of pliers and a pair of tweezers: the basic design is similar, but we put them to completely different uses!

A pair of scissors is not one simple machine, but two different simple machines combined – a compound machine. Each blade is a wedge, but it's also working as a lever. The fulcrum is the point where the blades join. When you bring the handles of the scissors together, the force pushes the blades together to make the cut.

A pair of pliers has blunt ends instead of blades. Pliers have longer arms for the handle and shorter arms for the wedges.

You make a large movement with your hand, which puts a lot of force into a small movement, enabling a strong grip.

Tweezers have the fulcrum at one end instead of the middle. They are useful when you don't need to use a lot of force, but want to make a precise movement. Because of the location of the fulcrum, the tweezers don't amplify the force you apply.

Five top uses for simple machines

Opening and closing things. You use a simple machine whenever you use a screw-top lid, on drinks and shampoo bottles, toothpaste tubes and hundreds of other things.

Levering things. Whenever you use a screwdriver or coin to open the battery compartment of a toy, you're using a lever.

Moving! We use wheels and axles all the time, from bicycles to buses and trains to trolleys. On a car or a bus, the wheels aren't just on the outside: the steering wheel is another wheel, and the cogs and gears inside the engine are wheels, too.

Cutting things. Almost everything you cut, you cut with a wedge. The knife you use for food, the scissors you use for paper and fabric, and even the teeth in your mouth. Wedges push through tough or flexible stuff by forcing a way between its fibres or particles.

Holding things together. If you pin a picture to a wall, the pin is a wedge; if you nail something together, the nail is a wedge; if you screw something together, the screw is – obviously – a screw!

Did you kNow?

The bones in your body act as levers and your joints act as pivots, or fulcrums, for the levers. Your muscles provide the effort to move loads. The load can be part of your body, or something you are carrying, kicking or pushing.

You have all three types of lever in your body:

When you nod your head, the load is its weight, the fulcrum is the point where the top of your spine meets your skull, and the effort is provided by the muscles at the back of your neck. It's a class 1 lever because the fulcrum is positioned between the effort and the load.

When you stand on tiptoe, your toes are the fulcrum. The load is the weight of your body. The effort is provided by the muscles in your calf.

The load and effort are on the same side of the fulcrum, with the load closest to it so it's a class 2 lever.

When you bend your arm to lift something, the fulcrum is your elbow. The effort is provided by your biceps muscle, which attaches to a bone in the forearm close to the elbow. The load is carried in the hand, at the far end of the forearm. The effort is closer to the fulcrum than the load so this is a class 3 lever.